Shagging for America

(UNWRITTEN RULES FOR UNREPENTANT MALES)

BY SAM PRIEST

ILLUSTRATED BY JAMES ANGUS

COPYRIGHT 2001 HANGOVER MEDIA, INC.

Published by:
Hangover Media, Inc.
65 Reade St., 5th Fl.
New York, NY   10007

T: 212.732.2277
F: 212.964.8026
E: chris@sheckys.com

Written by: Sam Priest
All Illustrations by: James Angus
Cover and Content Design/Layout by: Greg Evans

www.shaggingforamerica.com

Copyright 2001 by Hangover Media, Inc.
1st Edition
ISBN 0-9662658-9-0
Printed in the United States

To: A.K., N.W., C.B., C.F., B.E., C.V.F., C.H., K.M. and all of the beautiful women of New York.

TABLE OF CONTENTS

CHAPTER 1

WOMEN ARE PSYCHOTIC

DON'T TRY TO UNDERSTAND WOMEN. You can't. They don't understand themselves. Instead of tormenting yourself over some incomprehensible act committed by your girlfriend, just remember this simple truth.

Women are psychotic.

Even the most beautiful woman doesn't feel beautiful most of the time. She feels her beauty is something separate that she carries around like a shawl or a purse. She likes to dress well and have beautiful accessories, because she wants to make these things part of her, like her skin or make-up or hair. If you tell a woman she has nice skin, it's like telling her she has a nice handbag. It makes her feel good, but she's not really sure it's her that you are complimenting.

A woman can feel detached from her body in a way that men generally don't. Even normal women can feel this way. But watch out for anorexics or bulimics. They feel this way all the time.

A woman doesn't know what you are thinking when you look at her. Therefore, compliments can be perceived as something quite abstract. But God help you if you don't make them because she wants to think that the purse, her skin, her clothes, eye make-up and hair and yes, even her soul, are all one and the same thing and she will feel equally prickly about your reaction to all of them.

WHAT WOMEN WANT

Scientists have found that women respond well to certain things. In no particular order, here are 20 of them.

1. Any indication that you might be interested in staying with her for a long time.
2. Flowers (a sign of 1)
3. Compliments of any kind (also a sign of 1)
4. Attention and more attention (yet again a sign of 1)
5. Indications that you like children or would like to have children

with her (yet again a sign of 1)

6. Indications from you that she has lost weight (another sign of 1 above)

7. Letting her decorate your apartment (see 1 above)

8. Expensive jewelry (a sign of commitment – see 1 above)

9. Expensive shoes (ditto)

10. Expensive clothes (ditto)

11. Expensive dinners (ditto)

12. Men who stay awake for at least 5 minutes after sex

13. Extended foreplay (1 again)

14. Money (good genes)

15. Power (good genes)

16. Fame (good genes)

17. Charisma (good genes)

18. Good looks (good genes)

19. Deep masculine voice (good genes)

20. Tight butt (good jeans)

Keep in mind that items 7 through 11 and 14 can cost you money. So go with the others if you can!

PAY NO ATTENTION TO WHAT WOMEN SAY. What they want is 1 through 20 above.

HAPLESS MEN OFTEN ASK:

"What did she mean when she said _____?"

The true shagger's response is always the same. "Why are you wasting your time listening to her when you could be using the time to plan next week's shagging schedule?"

WHAT WOMEN DON'T WANT

These same scientists have found that women don't like the following five things:

1. Thinking you might not be interested in staying with her for a long time.
2. Thinking it was a one night stand (i.e., you won't be there to raise the child).
3. Thinking or being reminded that you or someone else might think she is fat.
4. Thinking you are boring or stupid or poor or stingy or physically inadequate and therefore have lousy genes that she is wasting her time on.
5. Not providing her with 1 - 20 above.

8

CHAPTER 2

SHAGGING – SPORT, ART OR SCIENCE?

SHAGGING HAS MANY QUALITIES OF SPORT.

For example, you keep score.

At times it can even resemble professional wrestling.

But it also has characteristics of both science and art.

A good shagger must understand the biology and psychology of the female and be an artist at using this knowledge against her.

There are two important scientific principles necessary to understanding women.

The first is the Biological Imperative:

Women wish to marry the rich and famous guy and have children with him who will inherit the money.

The second is the Psychological Imperative:

Women wish to marry the rich and famous guy and have children with him who will inherit the money.

Women state these two propositions differently. They say:

"I just want to be loved for me."

They leave out: "By a rich and famous guy."

But they mean the same thing.

NO!!!   YES!!!   NO!!!

Under 18, 18-35, and over 35.

TYPES OF WOMEN

WHILE WOMEN COME in many sizes, shapes and forms, they are basically divided into two classes:

1. Women under 35

AND

2. Women over 35

What do you need to know about women over 35?
Nothing. Simply avoid them at all costs.

HOW CAN YOU TELL IF A WOMAN IS OVER 35?

WOMEN ALWAYS LIE about their age, so asking will not help. Other methods must be used.

You may have to ransack her apartment for clues.

First, look through her purse for her driver's license. NOTE: smart women over 35 are onto this trick and never carry a driver's license.

Second, ask all her girl friends. They are dying to tell you.

Third, write to the Department of Motor Vehicles for a copy of her driver's license. (You will need to find out her last name to do this.)

Fourth, request a duplicate copy of her birth certificate from the appropriate local administrative authority.

Fifth, Premorin or other medication for the symptoms of menopause in the bathroom cabinet is a bad sign.

What you need to know about women under 35:

Two primary characteristics predominate among women under 35:

1. Massive insecurity

2. A desire to get married and have children.

And no wonder they feel insecure—they're constantly being judged on how they look.

What you need to know about women over 35:

Two primary characteristics predominate among single women over 35:

1. Massive insecurity

2. A desire to get married and have children *quickly.*

What you need to know if you meet a woman over 35:

Don't worry, the nearest subway stop is probably less than 10 blocks away.

MARRIED MEN MAY ASK:

"Is this book for me?"

Yes. It can help freshen your marriage by motivating you to have sex with other women.

(Not that you need any motivation.)

Always Keep Score.

CHAPTER 5

KEEPING SCORE

ALL GREAT SHAGGERS keep score (even if they pretend they don't). Here's how it's done.

Number of Shagging Points:

1. Blow Job = .50
2. Sexual Intercourse = 1.00
3. Up the Gurgler = 1.50
4. Either 2 or 3 above and you shave her pussy (unless she is over 35, in which case you get no credit because she is desperate and will let you do anything) = 2.00

B.J.'s are valued at only half a point because many women will give them to avoid having sex with you.

One important difference between men and women is that women tend to play for a low score.

NOTE: There is no credit for doing these activities with a man.

SOME FREQUENTLY ASKED QUESTIONS ABOUT KEEPING SCORE

Do prostitutes count?

Yes, prostitutes count. But like dynamite fishing, sleeping with prostitutes is considered unsportsmanlike.

Do women over 35 count?

Yes, but this is also unsportsmanlike.

Is it necessary for you to have an orgasm?

Somewhere along the way, yes. Otherwise why are you doing this?

Do you get credit for sleeping with the same girl twice?

No. You cannot accumulate more than 2.0 points with any one girl. Once you have had sex with a girl, you are finished with that girl for that activity. Of course, you can always go back and give her one up the gurgler if you missed it the first time around. But, in general, there are no extra points for sleeping with the same girl twice.

Remember: we don't want you getting trapped in a relationship. Relationships can lead to low scores and, in extreme cases, marriage.

What's a good score?

It depends a little on your age. For example, President John

Fitzgerald Kennedy, one of the great all time shaggers, is believed to have scored only a bit over 1,000 points due to his untimely death at the age of 47.

George Simenon and Warren Beatty, the two top shaggers of the 20th century, are believed to have each scored more than 10,000 shagging points. Both Beatty and Simenon are now retired. Simenon retired shortly after his death. Beatty retired when he got married and started having sex with women over 35.

SHAGGING POINTS CHART	
LIFETIME POINTS	WHAT IT MEANS
0-10	You are a woman and probably a nun
10-20	You are asexual
20-50	Novice
50-100	Getting there
100-500	Respectable
500-1,000	Yessiree Bob!
1,000-5,000	Accomplished shagger
over 5,000	You are Charlie Sheen
over 10,000	You are Warren Beatty
over 15,000	You are a fucking liar

Protect your sperm at all times

"I use them to masturbate"

CHAPTER 6

SHAGGING EQUIPMENT

NOW THAT YOU KNOW how to keep score, here's some tips on how to get started.

Very little equipment is actually needed for successful shagging. The following is a list of things to bring on every date.

1. Half a dozen condoms
2. 1 small bottle of Astro-glide (a lubricant, in case your date is frigid)
3. A cell phone (so you can be called away to an urgent appointment immediately after having sex)

4. One Gillette Mach Three razor (to shave her pussy)

Protect your sperm at all times.

Condoms are important for two reasons:

1. They can prevent disease.
2. They can prevent years of unwanted child support obligations. However, they don't work if you don't wear them.

Caveat! One great shagger I know came out of the bathroom after a great bout of sex and went back into the bedroom to discover to his horror that his girlfriend had retrieved his used condom from the garbage and was furiously rubbing its contents into her vagina.

Another shagger was brought down by a woman who rifled his pockets before they had sex and removed his condoms replacing them after she had poked numerous holes in them with a pin. Now the poor guy has three children.

Your sperm is precious. Make sure it stays in the condom and make sure the condom stays in the garbage. If necessary, throw it out the window. In a pinch, feed it to her dog. Then throw the dog out the window.

STRIPPER

MODEL

ACTRESS

JOURNALIST

24

CHAPTER 7

WHAT KIND OF WOMAN SHOULD I DATE?

NOW THAT YOU HAVE THE EQUIPMENT, you need to decide whom to date.

Fortunately, there is a clear hierarchy of women. From most to least desirable, the top three classes of women to date are:

1. Strippers

2. Models

3. Movie stars

Strippers are ranked number one for obvious reasons.

Models are better than movie stars because they are younger and almost always better looking.

If you are not rich, famous and good looking or don't live in Manhattan, you may have to be content with dating civilians. This is not recommended. However, if you must do so, here is the ranking of civilian women in order of desirability.

1. Girls who work for Conde Nast
2. Girls who work for Calvin Klein
3. Girls who work in Chelsea art galleries
4. Ballet dancers
5. Girls who work at Sothebys
6. Struggling actresses
7. Girls who go to Juilliard
8. Girls who go to Parsons
9. Struggling waitresses
10. Girls who go to FIT
11. College girls who moonlight as dominatrixes

12. Other college girls

13. Nurses

14. Married women under 35

15. East Village girls

16. Prostitutes

17. Homeless women

18. Blind girls

19. Women attorneys

20. Socialites from the Upper East Side

21. Heroin addicts

22. Women in the fashion business who are not models and don't work for Conde Nast or Calvin Klein

23. Women over 35

24. Women who don't live in Manhattan

25. Women journalists

*"May I buy you a drink or would you prefer it if
I just gave you the money instead?"*

CHAPTER 8

MEETING WOMEN

ONE OF THE MOST IMPORTANT RULES of successful shagging is that if you want to sleep with a girl, you must talk to her first.

Meeting women is not difficult. Unless you live in Libya or outside of Manhattan, they are everywhere. You have only to reach out and grab one.

Here's how:

The hard way. Picking up girls in bars.

This is the social equivalent of cold calling.

No matter how charming your lines, a lot of women are going to hang up. After all, you could be a serial killer, or worse yet, out for a one night stand.

When picking up girls in bars it is best to work as a team. This means you will need at least one friend. If you are reading this book and you don't have any friends, I can't say I'm surprised.

Let's assume you have a friend named Andrew.

You approach two girls who are total strangers.

"Have you met my friend Andrew?"

Now that one of you has been introduced, improvise.

If you must fly solo, here's some hints.

Approach your target.

"May I be the first to say how attractive you look this evening?"

If she takes this as a compliment, she is dumb, which is probably the best thing you could hope for.

If she says, "You're not the first," you may have an interesting challenge ahead of you.

Another possibility is to ask: "May I buy you a drink or would you prefer it if I just gave you the money instead?"

If she doesn't laugh, walk away quickly.

Be careful of the lighting
in bars. While hall of fame
shaggers never go to bed with an
ugly woman, they sometimes
wake up next to one.

"I'm Harrison Ford's younger brother"

CHAPTER 9

GOOD PARTIES

PARTIES ARE KEY. Go to lots of good parties.

At parties, you can be introduced to women. You can also approach them far more easily because they will be less on guard.

Since people will assume you were invited, you have instant credibility simply for being at the party.

This is especially true of good parties.

Good parties are defined as parties which are at least 10 percent celebrities and 20 percent models.

Since you will never be invited to parties like this, you must learn how to crash them.

This involves another useful skill which all great shaggers must perfect, namely, lying.

There are three or four proven techniques for crashing good parties.

First, try masquerading as someone who is invited.

Find out the name of someone else who is invited and say you are him. You can do this by asking friends or by peering over someone else's shoulder at the guest list.

Be prepared for minor embarrassment in the unlikely event that the doorman actually knows the person you are claiming to be.

Second, masquerade as a friend or close relative of a celebrity.

Celebrities are automatically invited to everything. The doorman will not want to offend a friend or close relative of a celebrity.

But remember, pick someone who might remotely fit your persona.

For example, if you are Caucasian, do not say you are Puff Daddy's younger brother.

However, if you go to enough parties as Harrison Ford's kid brother, everyone will start believing it.

All doormen know each other. So once you have established yourself, you will get in almost every time.

Or try masquerading as a gossip columnist or society photographer. HINT: If you are claiming to be a photographer you must carry a camera.

This is also an identity you can use over and over again.

Once a few doormen get to know you, you are golden.

Now that you are in, you need only harvest the guests.

Show no fear. Keep lying at all costs. Remember that the truth is your enemy. And never admit anything.

If your squash buddy from work walks over and says "Hello Sam" while you are chatting up a Ford model pretending to be Texas oil billionaire David Koch, simply look at him like he is out of his mind, turn your back and continue.

He will get the idea.

CHAPTER 10

SURROUND YOURSELF WITH GIRLS

WOMEN ARE LIKE LEMMINGS. They are attracted to men who already have lots of women.

So always go out with a pack of attractive women.

If you don't have a pack of attractive women, find one.

Say you spot a group of five gorgeous models conversing in the VIP room of an exclusive nightclub. Go over and stand in the middle of them.

If they ask what you are doing, say you are "waiting for a friend." If they start looking around for a bouncer, tell them your friend is Harvey Weinstein. Then strike up a conversation.

Even if they refuse to talk to you for more than 30 seconds, everyone else will think you know them.

This will make the other girls in the place much more open to talking to you.

And don't think they didn't notice. Women notice everything. Fortunately, they can rarely workout what it all means.

Try to remember her name.

CHAPTER 11

DATING

THE FIRST RULE of first dates is that anything you say can and will be used against you.

She will be looking for clues that you are ambitious, successful and considerate, confident, like your job and are interested in her.

Since it is unlikely that you are any of these things, the safest course on the first date is to say nothing. In fact, if you are reading this book, you're probably an idiot. So keep your mouth shut.

Instead, your job is to figure out whether it is worth the effort of getting into her panties. Once you decide it is, you will need clues to what will get you there.

Let her talk and keep the drinks coming. Get as much alcohol into her as possible. Nod your head or say "uh-huh" occasionally if necessary to stay awake.

If you have trouble listening, bring a tape recorder. Listen to it later.

Or don't listen to it at all. It doesn't matter.

If you must talk, tell jokes or compliment her or her appearance. You can also ask questions. But never reveal anything personal.

Meanwhile, you are listening for valuable clues. Ask her where she was when JFK was assassinated. If she remembers, she is over 35. Ask her if she has ever been attracted to another woman. If she says yes, you may have threesome potential.

And get physical. Touch her hand, waist or arm. Affectionately brush her hair out of your drink. Touching her at every reasonable opportunity will get your date used to your physical presence.

Excessive touching can be annoying. Be sensitive to her reactions. If she grimaces and playfully tosses her drink in your face or calls the police, this is a sign that you have gone too far too soon.

Always make sure the place you are going is within two or three blocks of your house. If necessary, move to Soho. When she is drunk enough for you to touch her breasts without flinching, you can pop the question.

"I'd like you to see my [apartment, loft]. It's just around the corner. A quick drink and we'll call it a night."

She will be curious but won't trust either you or herself, so she may need some cajoling. The best way to pop the question is when you come up for air after a long tongue kiss. Always keep one hand firmly inside her vagina while you are asking.

How many dates should I schedule for the same evening?

Always schedule at least three dates for every free evening. This way you are likely to end up with at least one girl who won't cancel. If the other two don't cancel, you can always cancel them at the last minute.

Work is always a good excuse.

WHY ARE WOMEN SO UNRELIABLE ABOUT DATING?

Women cancel dates for many reasons. Here are a few:

1. They can't stand you and were only being polite when you asked them out in the first place. This is not a good sign.
2. They aren't ready to have sex with you yet and are afraid of what might happen if they show up. This is a very good sign.
3. To see if you are interested enough to call them again.
4. They got a better offer for the evening.
5. They completely forgot.
6. They are dating your boss.

For those of you who don't know any better, they are not doing the laundry, washing their hair, going to the gym or comforting a heartsick girlfriend. These are lies.

But whatever her excuse for canceling at least you'll have two backups.

DATING TIP: Try to remember your date's name. This is especially important during sex. This involves keeping good records. It is worth investing in a Palm Pilot.

There is nothing worse than spending an evening with a woman whose name you can't remember, but whom you have on the tip of your tongue. Try writing your date's name on a piece of paper. Keep it in your pocket so you can check it periodically during dinner.

When you put a girl's name in your phone book, always make a little notation of something to remember her by. Otherwise, three months later you will be racking your brains to figure out who she is. Little hints, like "big tits" or "works at Fendi" can be invaluable reminders later on.

To become a hall of fame shagger you must master the art of going out on a first date, getting her back to your apartment by 10p.m. and out the door before Letterman comes on at 11:30p.m.

Don't kid yourself. This requires careful planning.

Having maneuvered your date into bed at 10:30 and at 11:00 having begun to endure her telling you how this has never happened to her before, that she never sleeps with a man until at least the 10th date, you can then quietly agree, "In fact, I make it a point never to sleep with a girl on the first date."

If it is her apartment, you will then be able to slide quickly off the bed and into your clothes and a waiting taxi before she recovers.

If you are both at your apartment, an additional hint may be required.

"What's that noise outside?" you inquire, quickly sitting up and slipping into your pants.

"I didn't hear anything."

"Yes, thought so. It's your taxi waiting. Well, love, I guess I'll see you around."

This approach, while it does involve a certain amount of physical danger, will generally save you the trouble of having to speak to her ever again.

This is the good news.

Women generally give up easily. If you do not return her calls for a few weeks you are unlikely to hear from her again.

"He just needs time."

CHAPTER 12

IT'S NOT ABOUT YOU

NEVER TAKE IT personally if a woman doesn't like you. It's not about you.

A woman will like you if you say and do things that she thinks are in her interest. If you show that you are not interested in what she wants (attention, presents, marriage and children), she will quickly lose interest in you. She may even think you are a bad person or at best a worthless cad.

Since you are reading this book, you are unlikely to have any interest in marriage, children or buying her expensive gifts. You will have to feign interest in these matters. If you do it well, you will be regarded as a very attractive man.

Fortunately for you, many women have an unlimited capacity for self delusion. She will filter what you say in order to hear what she wants to hear. This means she will believe it when you fake an interest in marriage and children. In fact, even if you tell her from the beginning that you have no interest in a serious relationship, she won't believe it. She'll tell her girlfriends that you "just need time."

Even if you tell her that you broke up with your last 57 girlfriends because you had no interest in marriage and they did, she will rationalize it. She will tell herself that you just weren't interested in marrying the other 57 girls. But of course, you might be interested in marrying *her*.

Date Anorexics.

CHAPTER 13

SHAGGING ON THE CHEAP

A MASSIVE SHAGGING CAMPAIGN can be massively expensive. The trick is to do it on the tight budget.

There is a simple test for determining whether you are spending too much money on dates. It works almost anywhere in the world. A date should never cost more than an hour with a good-looking hooker. In New York, $200 is your limit.

For the first few dates, go to free events. Preferably parties with free food and drinks. You can have a great time, not spend a dime and keep an eye out for future prospects.

Avoid dates at mealtimes. If your date extends into the dinner hour leave abruptly citing work, another appointment you just remembered or any cell phone call that happens to come in around this time. If you do meet at mealtimes, say you have already eaten.

Better yet, have her cook you a meal.

Although she may be a lousy cook, you are unlikely to get a check afterwards.

Try to meet for a drink, a movie or a free event for the first few dates. On average, accomplished shaggers can get a girl into bed on the strength of just one moderately priced restaurant meal.

Women sometimes feel vaguely cheated if they don't get a free meal out of you. If you do have to buy dinner, eat two hot dogs before you go out, then pretend to be on a strict diet.

Eat the bread and butter and one appetizer. This will reduce the cost of dinner by 40%. And with any luck, she will order a salad.

Dating anorexics is also a good idea. At least they won't hold you up for a big meal. Beware of bulimics. They will gorge themselves on expensive dishes and throw them up in the ladies room when you least suspect it. Besides, bulimics have bad breath.

CHAPTER 14

BEWARE OF "BUNNY BOILERS"

THE BAD NEWS is that a small percentage of women are obsessive stalker types or "Bunny Boilers." Bunny Boilers will continue to call and may even wait for hours outside your home or office trying to see you, even though you have made it clear that it was just a one night stand.

Bunny Boilers take the fun out of shagging.

Here are a few simple rules to help you avoid obsessive stalkers.

Never give out your home phone number to a woman until you are engaged or married to her. Instead, get a voicemail box where a caller can leave messages. You can tell her it's a phone, but you just don't answer because you "have a thing about phones." You can also give out your cell phone number. Cell phone numbers and service providers are easily changed.

Since obsessive stalker types are often over 35, you can avoid many of them by not dating older women.

How can you tell if you are dating a Bunny Boiler?

- If your caller ID shows that she called you 11 times in 10 minutes but didn't leave a message.
- If she talks a lot about litigation she is involved in or boyfriends who have orders of protection, watch out.
- If you have a sense you are being followed and you keep running into her in public places, you are in big trouble.
- If you come home and find your pet rabbit floating in a pot on the stove, you are dating a Bunny Boiler.

If you discover you are dating a Bunny Boiler, there are a few things you can do.

Get an order of protection.

Call the police. They won't do anything but calling them will make you feel better.

In extreme cases, move to Europe.

This may also allow your reputation to gradually recover.

"Hello darling. How about dinner tonight?"

CHAPTER 15

MASTERING THE SHORT TERM RELATIONSHIP ("STR")

HOW LONG SHOULD A RELATIONSHIP LAST?

Just as having great sex should take no more than three minutes, the ideal relationship lasts exactly three weeks.

How many relationships should I carry on at the same time?

You should generally carry on five three week relationships at once.

Three weeks is the most convenient duration for a relationship. More humane than the one night stand, the three week relationship will enable you to achieve high scores and a measure of enjoyment that comes from getting to know someone superficially.

In three weeks you can:

1. Have three or four dinner dates
2. Shag her rotten several times
3. Spend an entire weekend together
4. Go to one movie
5. Never have a conversation that goes beyond the superficial
6. Break up painlessly (see "Exit Strategy")

And if you are really enjoying it, what the hell! You can even extend it for another week. (Remember convenience is the key to any successful relationship.)

All without the need to meet her parents, discuss children or marriage, look at pictures of her as a child or go to a friend's wedding. All these things and more can be avoided. With any luck, she need not even find out your home phone number or what you really do for a living.

During a STR, she will still be on her best behavior, since she doesn't know you very well. Which is how you want to keep it.

You can carry on up to five STR's simultaneously. Don't attempt more than five. Even if you have a Palm Pilot, you will get confused.

With five girls on the go, you can schedule one or two dates with each every week and still have at least two days free to find more girls. Sunday nights must be kept free to make phone calls.

Pick three nights – say Monday, Wednesday and Saturday.

Call each girl on Sunday night. Schedule a dinner with Alexa (Upper East Side heiress) for Monday, drinks with Doris (starving East Village artist/waitress) on Wednesday, dinner with Uta (the Swedish model) also on Wednesday and a movie on Saturday with Karin (struggling socialite) and also with Larisa (the beautiful Russian with no visible means of support).

Remember you can and should cancel any date that later becomes inconvenient.

If it turns out there is a party for Ford models on Wednesday night at the Puck building, simply cancel Doris and Uta and go to the party.

They will both be intrigued that you cancelled them and will actually like you more for it.

Don't worry. Doris could never get invited to the Ford party. Uta might, except that she works for Elite and probably won't go.

Your schedule leaves you four free evenings. Sunday night to make phone calls to schedule the next week's activities, and Tuesday, Thursday and Friday to go to parties and find more girls.

With five three week relationships, unless you extend one or two for a week, on average you will have to replace all five girls every 15 weeks. This can easily be accomplished by going to good parties and following the tips in this book. In fact, your problem is likely to be keeping your list down to five at any one time.

DEALING WITH "RULES GIRLS"

The system works even with girls who do "The Rules." In general, we recommend avoiding "Rules Girls."

A Rules Girl uses tactics to stall you at second base until she can figure out whether you are really marriage material. You will spend more money per shagging point with a Rules Girl. This is inefficient.

The good news is that very few women are capable of sticking to the Rules. And since you are scheduling three dates a night anyway, you can always fit a Rules Girl in once or twice a week. If you haven't scored at least half a point in the first six weeks, dump her.

One easy way to break down a Rules Girl is to buy her a fake engagement ring. However, for legal reasons, it is best to propose to her under an assumed name.

Once you have gotten a Rules Girl into the sack, the Rules will start working for you. The best approach is never to call her again. (After all, we don't want to encourage women to do The Rules.) Since the Rules don't allow a Rules Girl to call you, if you don't call her you are off scott-free!

The definition of Eternity:
the time between your coming and her going.

CHAPTER 16

THE 2-3-11 RULE

HOW OFTEN should I see my girlfriend or mistress?

There is an easy to remember rule for determining the frequency of contact between you and your girlfriends.

It's called the 2-3-11 Rule. The 2-3-11 Rule works like this:

2. Never see your girlfriend two days in a row.

3. Always call her at least once every three days.

11. See her (and, if possible, shag her) at least once every eleven days.

Scientists have proven that if you do not see your girlfriend at least once every 11 days, she will think you have broken up with her and that you are no longer in a relationship. This is dangerous, because it means she won't have sex with you anymore. Therefore you must call her every three days and give her a proper seeing to every 11 days.

Using the 2-3-11 Rule, you can keep up to eleven girls on the go at the same time (and more if you can find the time to shag two girls or more per day). However, a note of caution. These quantities may not be achievable by a married man with a full-time job who lives with his wife.

"Hello Darlings."

CHAPTER 17

SHOW NO FEAR

THE FIRST RULE of successful serial dating is to show no fear and treat them like dogs.

Remember you are strong, self-confident and funny. You don't need any woman, no matter how beautiful, poised, intelligent or rich. Instead they need you. It is a privilege for her to talk to you.

Even though this is not remotely the truth, you must act as though it was.

You must be fearless. You must make them love you for making them beg.

You must walk up to large groups of models you have never met and crack jokes until they are doubled over with laughter.

You must touch your date as though you owned her body.

You must look through her with the intensity of a laser beam.

You must tell her what you are going to do to her when you get home.

You must keep pushing the sexual intensity of the conversation until she begins to feel totally out of control.

Run your hand over her face and your thumb over her lips.

Gently penetrate her mouth with your thumb.

Then abruptly get up and announce that you have to leave immediately because it is time for your daily tantric exercise routine. Tell her you want to see her again but that she is not to make the mistake of wearing panties next time.

CHAPTER 18

YOU ARE NEVER TOO OLD OR TOO UGLY TO SHAG WOMEN UNDER 35

AGE DOES NOT MATTER. You're a guy.

Every man at some point in his life has a moment when he realizes that it used to be harder on the way out than it is now going in.

Don't despair. You are never too old to shag women under 35. Even if you look at a Playboy magazine and think "I remember sex" there is still hope.

Even if you are 87 years old and your shirt front is covered with drool, you can still go out with women under 35.

But it will cost you.

BLIND DATES

The blind date is the best solution for the old or ugly man.

By dating blind girls you are not only having fun, you are committing an act of charity. In some cases, your dates could even be tax deductible (consult your tax advisors).

"Get lost!"

CHAPTER 19

NEVER GIVE AWAY GIRLS

IT DOESN'T MATTER how many girls you know. Never let any of your friends near them. Make them beg for introductions.

After all, what's in it for you? Of course, if they offer a tidy sum in cash, that's different.

Let's say you're a lawyer. For your best clients, one introduction for every $250,000 of business would be about right.

Non-cash consideration is also acceptable. If you are a writer, it is a good idea to keep your publisher happy. Introduce him to as many girls as possible.

CHAPTER 20

IF SHE WON'T TAKE HER CLOTHES OFF, TAKE YOURS OFF

PARTICULARLY ON A FIRST DATE, you may find yourself in a futile wrestling match with your date as you try to get her top or bra off.

Instead of wasting valuable minutes struggling with your date's clothing, simply stand up, slip off your shirt and drop your trousers. Then resume struggling with her clothing.

This will put her at a distinct disadvantage. Since you are already naked, she will have to leave quickly or give in to your relentless advances.

If she leaves, you can use the valuable time you saved in trying to cajole her into the sack to schedule another girl for the rest of the evening.

WHAT TO DO WHEN SHE SAYS "NO"

When a girl says "no", it rarely means "no", but it might mean she wants to take a short break.

If you have three fingers inside her, are wrestling with her bra with your free hand and have your tongue buried in her right ear, she may begin to find it all a bit much for a first date.

When she starts saying "No, stop" and squirms away, let her do so. Gracefully get up and mix a couple of more drinks.

Talk for a bit. If you both smoke, have a cigarette.

After about five minutes, resume making out.

You will get even further this time.

When she gets uncomfortable and starts breathlessly again with the "don't," and the "stop," ease up and kiss her gently. Take the pressure off for a few minutes.

She will be grateful because you listened and responded. But don't give her enough respite to start thinking about ending the evening.

In fact, you should quickly resume your attentions more forcefully than ever.

Keep this up until you get the full point.

Always keep a box of toothbrushes handy.

CHAPTER 21

WHAT IF SHE SPENDS THE NIGHT?

IF YOU DECIDE to let her spend the night, you will have to be prepared to alter your normal routine.

Lying down fully dressed with a few beers lined up on the night table, having a wank and falling into an all night snoring bout with the TV on may not work when she is sleeping over.

You may want to consider brushing your teeth, skipping the beers and taking your clothes off before you get into bed.

If you really want to go all out, light a few candles in the bedroom and pick up as many of the dirty socks and underwear as you can find.

In addition to the basic shagging equipment (condoms, Astroglide and Gillette Mach III razor), there is also some additional equipment you will need if she sleeps over:

1. Fresh 100% cotton **t-shirts**. While you may want to keep her warm by massaging her breasts all night, she will want to sleep in a thick clean t-shirt or maybe one of your white shirts from work.

2. Keep a box of **toothbrushes** under the sink in the bathroom. One of you will probably not want her to use your toothbrush. A note of caution. If you ever let her into your apartment again, the first thing she will do is check whether "her" toothbrush is still there. If it isn't, be prepared for problems. If it has been replaced by another girl's toothbrush and there are obvious lipstick marks on it, you should be prepared for physical violence.

3. **Tampons**. Always have a box on hand since her period will come on unexpectedly if you don't. Given the price of good sheets these

days, this is a worthwhile investment. If she asks why you have them, say you're sister left them at the apartment. (It's always good to have a sister.)

4. **Hairdryer** and **brush**. She will want these in the morning.

5. **Massage oil**. In case you can convince her to give you one.

"It feels bigger in the dark."

CHAPTER 22

SHAGGING ETIQUETTE

HERE ARE SOME BASIC rules of shagging etiquette.

Should you know a woman's last name before having sex with her?

Definitely not.

If you have had sex with her, she may even want to change her last name to yours.

While this would make it easier to remember her name, it is not a reason to get married.

How long should sex take?

Three minutes maximum. (Remember, you have work to do.)

What to say after sex if she doesn't have an orgasm:

"Hey baby, I got mine, you get yours!"

What to say if she comes home from a weekend trip and finds a used condom in the garbage:

"I use them to masturbate."

What to say if you've just had wild sex on the beach, but you don't feel like walking your date back to her car:

"So, I guess I'll see you around."

In etiquette, women seem to have everything backwards.

For example, men like to call a woman before they have had sex with her.

Strangely, women like a man to call her after he has had sex with her.

Should you call a woman the next day after you have had sex for the first time?

Answer: Proceed with caution.

If you do call, you are now in a relationship.

This means she will think it was not a one night stand.

She will even expect you to call her again. But this will give you the option to have sex with her again.

If you do not call, you now have a mortal enemy. She will also tell all her girlfriends what a bastard you are.

This will make it more difficult for you to shag them.

REMEMBER: Always stay on good terms with the women you have shagged.

When should you call?

A. Within one year
B. Within six months
C. Within 24 hours
D. Within 48 hours

The correct answer is (C) unless she is over 35, in which case you can afford to let her stew for another day.

What to do if you have a small penis?
Turn out the lights and tell her "It feels bigger in the dark."

HOW TO LOOK BETTER NAKED

Lighting is key. The dimmer the better.

Always stand with your back to the light source. Avoid overhead lighting.

It will reflect off your bald spot and make your stomach cast a shadow on the floor.

AFTER SEX

Always remove any ropes, gags or bondage equipment from your date before you fall asleep.

Also make sure the condom has been irretrievably disposed of. If she does not have a dog, throw it out the window.

If possible, get her out of the apartment before you fall asleep. That way she will not be able to go through your stuff for things to question you about or blackmail you with.

If it is her apartment, you will have to sleep in the cab on the way home.

If you have trouble staying awake for more than 30 seconds after sex, try smoking a cigarette. This should keep you awake for another 10 minutes. If it doesn't, call the Fire Department.

CHAPTER 23

EVERYTHING IS DENIABLE

IF YOUR GIRLFRIEND finds another girl's panties in the bed, don't panic. You can always deny it.

Relentless and uncompromising denials are effective even in the face of overwhelming evidence.

They were her panties and she just doesn't remember.

You bought them for her but got carried away and used them to masturbate.

The panties do not exist. She is just having another paranoid hallucination brought on by not eating enough.

If she catches you on her webcam having sex with another woman at your apartment, denying it is easy.

Just say: "It's not me." "I wasn't there." and/or "It must be someone else, I was out of town that day."

Never change your story no matter what.

CHAPTER 24

NEVER TELL A WOMAN YOU LOVE HER (EVEN IF YOU DON'T)

NEVER USE THE WORD "love" next to the word "you."

Once you tell her you love her, she's got you by the balls.

Or she will think she does.

By saying you love her you are creating expectations that you will not be able to control. You will constantly be asked to prove that you love her.

This means expensive gifts, and eventually an engagement ring. She will expect it all and the longer it takes to arrive, the angrier she will get.

Whether you mean it or not, telling a woman you love her will ruin your relationship. And once you've said it, it's too late to say "Just kidding."

However, if you are married, you can tell your wife you love her as a means of self preservation. Particularly if she is about to hit you with a blunt metal object.

Don't answer the door.

CHAPTER 25

NEVER LEAVE THE HOUSE ON VALENTINE'S DAY

VALENTINE'S DAY is a day that presents special problems for the accomplished shagger. Until our lobbyists succeed in having it abolished, here's how to handle this minefield of a day.

All of the women you are dating expect to be taken out and made a fuss over on Valentine's Day. If you don't, each one will realize that you are not serious about her. This means your girlfriends may lose interest in you.

Picking one girl to ask out will not work. All the others will probably dump you. Besides, if you do go out, you can easily be spotted by someone who knows one of your other girlfriends.

There is only one good solution to the Valentine's Day conundrum: *food poisoning*. Stay home in bed and tell all your girlfriends that you have a severe case of food poisoning. Use the time to plot out your shagging objectives for the next month.

Leave the phone on so you can convince well wishers not to come over and nurse you back to health. But don't answer the door under any circumstances in case one of them attempts this on their own initiative.

The next day you will be fresh from a good night's sleep and ready to resume your normal active shagging schedule. And think of all the money you will have saved.

86   *Buy the cheap ones.*

CHAPTER 26

FLOWERS ARE YOUR FRIEND

FLOWERS ARE YOUR FRIEND. Here's when to use flowers.
1. When your girlfriend has caught you in bed with her best friend.
2. When your girlfriend comes home from a two week vacation and finds another girl's panties under the covers.
3. After you cancelled your date with her for Saturday night on 30 minutes notice upon getting a last minute invitation to a Ford Models party at the Puck Building.

Flowers have many such defensive uses. But flowers can also be used offensively.
1. Show her how much you care in order to put her in the mood for a threesome.
2. To get her into bed more quickly (if you just started dating).

There is only one rule about flowers: *Buy the cheap ones!*

Often, she won't know the difference and, if she does, she'll forgive you because she will think you don't know the difference.

"Hey baby, I got mine. You get yours."

CHAPTER 27

FRIGIDITY — IT'S NOT YOUR PROBLEM

FRIGIDITY IS A PROBLEM for some women. The most important thing to remember is that it is easily overcome.

How can you tell if your date is frigid?

1. If she doesn't slide off her chair the minute you take off your shirt.
2. If she doesn't have an orgasm in the first five minutes of sex.

What do you do if your date is frigid?

First, be understanding.

Then, there are two schools of thought.

1. Offer to call her a taxi
2. Use the astroglide

You can have sex but not with her.

CHAPTER 28

WHAT YOU NEED TO KNOW ABOUT MENSTRUATION

IS IT OK TO HAVE SEX when she is having her period?

There are two schools of thought on this.

The first is that it is OK to have sex while your girlfriend is having her period, just not with her.

The second is that it is OK to have sex, but do it at her apartment. Otherwise your friends will think that a grenade went off in your bed.

CHAPTER 29

WHAT TO DO WHEN SHE GETS MAD

EVERY WOMAN you date is a time bomb. Eventually she is going to go off.

This is a good time to break up with her. But if you want to string her along for a few more weeks, here are ten ways to placate her.

1. Flowers (Buy the cheap ones.)
2. Tell her she has lost weight.
3. Take her shopping for a new pair of Manolo Blahniks (But be prepared. The madder she is, the more expensive the shoes will be.)
4. Tell her you didn't really mean it about wanting to have a threesome with her best friend.
5. Take your phone off the hook until it blows over.
6. Buy her a fake engagement ring. The cubic zirconium will fool her for weeks. But when she finds out you may have to move to another country.
7. Buy her any item of jewelry from Tiffany's, or buy her any other item of jewelry and put it in a Tiffany's box.
8. Give her a proper seeing to and stay awake afterwards.
9. Tell her how nice it would be to have a child with her.
10. Offer to throw out half of your pornography collection.

"*I'm moving to Uzbekistan.*"

CHAPTER 30

WHAT IF SHE GETS PREGNANT?

MANY SHAGGERS are in fear of that tearful yet expectant phone call asking for an immediate rendezvous. It can only mean one of two things:

1. She has the clap, or
2. She is pregnant.

In either case, it is bad news. If it is both, you are really in trouble.

Your first defense should be denial. After all, chances are it wasn't you.

Claim to be infertile from birth.

Say you have never had the clap in your life.

If she has been sleeping with anyone else, this will give her pause.

She won't be sure.

If she hasn't been sleeping with anyone else, she is likely to be more persistent.

Let's say you're having dinner with your girlfriend. Suddenly she looks at you and announces that she is pregnant. How you react is critical. Here are some possibilities.

1. Quietly and with dignity get up and leave the restaurant. When you get home, arrange for an unlisted phone number.
2. Casually ask who the father might be.
3. Offer to be helpful in locating the address of a nearby abortion clinic.
4. Sigh wistfully and remark how cruel it would be to bring a helpless child into "this wicked wicked world."
5. Mention that you have recently been diagnosed with leprosy.
6. Recount your long family history of serious and irreversible birth defects.
7. Tell her about the new job you have taken in Uzbekistan.

8. Tell her that your relationship really isn't working out. (Then see 1 above.)

9. Tell her how sorry you are and that you understand how ghastly she must feel.

10. Remind her how fat she will get.

If none of the above work, tell her that if she decides to keep the child you regret that you will not be able to see her ever again.

If that doesn't work, offer to pay for half the abortion.

Don't let her move in.

CHAPTER 31

CAN'T LIVE WITH 'EM, DON'T LIVE WITH 'EM

ONE OF THE MOST IMPORTANT RULES of successful shagging may seem self-evident.

DON'T LET HER MOVE INTO YOUR APARTMENT!

This rule is often overlooked with sometimes fatal consequences.

Letting her move in can lead to marriage, low scores and loss of interest in sex.

CHAPTER 32

MARRIAGE AND HOW TO AVOID IT

THERE ARE ONLY TWO THINGS to be said about marriage:

1. Don't do it!
2. Don't even think about doing it!

There are no exceptions to these rules.

Except one.

If she is very very rich and bisexual, it's OK to marry her. If you are already married, don't worry. All is not lost. But you probably have a few questions. For example:

As a married man should you continue to have sex with your wife?

Mammals living under severe stress quickly lose interest in sex. That's why there is no sex after marriage. Instead, you should keep your marriage fresh by having sex with other women. Particularly, women under 35.

What if she asks you to marry her?

The important thing is to remain gravely non-committal. Under no circumstances should you nod or shake your head. Instead, keep your head moving in a slow circular motion until after she has stopped talking.

The other approach is to say nothing and look at your feet until she gives up and leaves the room.

Offer to wear a blindfold.

CHAPTER 33

HOW TO GET HER TO HAVE A THREESOME

THE FEMALE'S RELUCTANCE to have a threesome with another attractive woman is one of the most difficult and intractable problems facing the modern male. This is often a problem that takes time and effort to overcome. You will have to confront and deal with the jealousy thing head on.

Possible solutions

1. Offer to wear a blindfold
2. Date only lesbians
3. Tell her the other girl is a transvestite
4. Convince her to drop ectasy with you, after which she will probably be willing to have a threesome with a Grizzly Bear.

CHAPTER 34

WORK COMES FIRST

BALANCING WORK and a successful shagging schedule is not always easy. If in doubt, err on the side of your career not your dating schedule. The more successful you are, the more shagging you will be doing.

Sure JFK, Warren Beatty and Muhammad Ali were all good looking in their peak shagging days. But the real reason women fell all over themselves to get at these men is that they were successful, powerful, famous and rich. But even if you are just another run of the mill short, fat, balding billionaire, fear not. You too can shag models and Hollywood stars.

Yes, even Ron Perelman can get a high profile date. Sure, Ellen Barkin may be past her sell-by date, but she still turns a few heads and keeps those journalists' pens moving.

The best way to attract women and raise your score is to have good things going on in your own life. If you are happy, successful and self-confident, your shagging will improve.

Keep looking at those feet.

CHAPTER 35

THE EXIT STRATEGY
("I GUESS I'LL SEE YOU AROUND")

THE TRULY ACCOMPLISHED SHAGGER spends very little time on actually seducing women. Rather, he focuses on a far more important concern. *Getting rid of them.*

It was a wise philosopher who first defined the concept of eternity. "Eternity," he said, "is the time between your coming and her going." A truer phrase was never written.

Dumping your date is the most important act in male-female relations and requires tact and consideration. There are two principal approaches to dumping your girl: the direct approach and the indirect approach. These approaches are not hassle free.

The Direct Approach:

Tell her you just discovered you have herpes.

The Indirect Approach:

Stop calling her and do not return her phone calls no matter what. NOTE: This will not work if you are living together.

There are many other examples of the indirect approach. The top ten are to:

1. Tell her the truth about what you do for a living.
2. Tell her you have contracted a rare skin disease and can no longer stand any sort of physical contact.
3. Admit that you are still married.
4. Ask her for her best friend's phone number because you would "like to ask her out."
5. Suggest you go "dutch" on your next date.
6. Leave another girl's panties in the bed.
7. Suggest a threesome with her sister or best friend.
8. Drop hints that you really are gay after all. Tell her she is very cute "for a girl" or sigh wistfully after sex and say "girls are OK, but they're not like the real thing."
9. Tell her that she looks fat.

10. Take the toilet seat off your toilet and hide it in the closet.

THE HASSLE-FREE BREAK-UP

When things start to get tense with one of your girlfriends, it is time for you to get going.

Here is an easy way to help her give herself the push with no effort on your part.

Let's say she walks in and gives you the usual spiel: "This relationship isn't going anywhere!"

You should say nothing and look intently at your feet.

She will continue: "There's really no point in our seeing each other anymore!"

Keep looking down. Remain silent.

Next she will say: "I want out. I'm getting nothing out of this relationship."

Keep staring at those shoes.

Finally she will explode: "That's it! I'm out of here!"

Don't look up until she has left the apartment.

CHAPTER 36

THE 20 SECRETS OF SUCCESSFUL SHAGGING

HERE'S WHAT WE HAVE LEARNED:

1. Always keep score.
2. Never date women over 35.
3. If you want to sleep with a girl, you must talk to her first.
4. If she won't take her clothes off, take yours off.

5. Date only strippers, models, actresses and girls who work for Conde Nast.

6. Beware of "Bunny Boilers."

7. Show no fear.

8. Never commit, never apologize.

9. Flowers are your friend.

10. Don't get married or engaged.

11. Everything is deniable.

12. There is no credit for sleeping with the same girl twice.

13. There is no sex after marriage (at least with your wife).

14. Never give out your home phone number.

15. Protect your sperm at all times.

16. Know what women want, don't listen to what they say.

17. Never tell a woman you love her even if you don't.

18. Always keep an eye on your exit strategy.

19. You are never too old or too ugly to shag women under 35.

20. Enjoy yourself at all times.

And remember,
be proud! You're
shagging for America.
The best damned
country in the
world!

Shagging Names